Ballet Apparel for Men

A Complete Beginner's Guide

David Hunter

Ballet For Men

Copyright Information

Hunter, David.

   Ballet apparel for men: A complete beginner's guide/ by David Hunter – 1st ed.

ISBN 978-1451557176

This book is part of a project by Ballet For Men.com

Follow Ballet For Men on Twitter, http://www.twitter.com/balletformen and

Facebook, http://www.facebook.com/pages/Ballet-For-Men/167172928402

Table of Contents

Introduction

Getting started in ballet can be hard. Especially for guys. Girls are often encouraged into dance and ballet. There are plenty of resources to get started in ballet, whether it is online or in a book, but most of it is directed toward girls. Information for male dancers is much harder to find. That is where this book comes in. It is specifically to help male dancers.

One of the first things that comes to the typical guy's mind when they think of ballet, is the tights. Guys don't usually wear tights, so this can be new and confusing. The exact apparel isn't required for the brand new dancer, but if you know about dance apparel for men, you will have less to be afraid of or confused about.

Once you do decide to make the step, and get equipped with all of the proper dance apparel, there is a bit to learn about. Finding out everything you need to know used to be hard. Now it is all available in one place, this book.

A Note for Parents of Young Dancers

The following has been written with teen or adult male dancers in mind. This is mainly because apparel is not so much of an issue for younger dancers. All of the following information can be applied to younger dancers, with perhaps the exception of the dance belt. For adult dancers, dance belts are worn under the tights and come in a thong back. For younger dancers, full back dance belts are available. These will be more comfortable for them, and perfect lines are not as important for younger dancers.

As your dancer gets older, he may receive guidance on attire from fellow dancers or teachers. However, this book can be a helpful resource for him when he becomes more independent. Congratulations on supporting your young dancer. There are many great opportunities for male dancers.

A Short Note on Masculinity and Dancing

In our society, men are typically supposed to be strong and tough. Dancing is not tough. It requires strength, but it does not make you tough. Fortunately, being a man isn't all about being tough. Part of being a man is being a human. Being a human is about expressing yourself. Expressing yourself requires you to occasionally not care what other people think about you. Doing what you want regardless of what other people think, whether you want to be or not, that will make you tough.

And for guys who are afraid of dancing because it isn't tough... how brave is it to be scared of dance?

A Long Note on Masculinity and Dancing

One of the first things that comes into a lot of people's mind when they think of men in ballet, seems to be about sexuality. I want to discuss this topic for that reason. In current American society, along with some other Western countries, this unspoken assumption is probably the number one thing preventing there being more men who take ballet classes.

If we rationally look at the origins of this "male dancers" stereotype, it loses much of its power. Allow me to get a bit social psychology here. In our society, there is not much of a definition of a real man. We do not have any cultural rule or practice that says what is expected of a boy in order to become a man. As a culture we base our definition of masculinity on what is presented through films, television, famous celebrities, rock, rap, and sports stars, and other media sources. I enjoy popular culture, but what does it give us as a definition of what a real man is?

It tells us that a 'Man' is a doer, a leader, he can get the job done. Give him a task, and he will do it. He'll score a touchdown and win the game. He'll beat the bad guys and save the day. He'll go to work and pay the bills. And he can do it all by himself, because he is a 'Man.' Something we don't see a real man do is express his emotions. He will not express fear, or he has failed. He will not express a need for someone else, or he has failed (unfortunately, one of the only culturally acceptable male expressions of emotion is aggression). And the real 'Man' definitely does not express beauty.

You can see how male dancing and men in ballet do not fit into this definition of a 'Man.' But in reality, that definition of men is far from the truth. It is fun to watch Bruce Willis kick around some bad guys, and you want him to win, but that is a myth and we live in reality. It is a reality where men are human and have human emotions to express. And many of us find that we want to express those emotions through dance and art. Because a man has the capacity to express himself, does not make him a failure.

It is easy to recognize this when it is broken down, but still the stereotypes or assumptions continue to either push males away from dance, or to just not offer the opportunity for men to dance. Many more men feel the need to dance than actually fulfill that need.

The assumptions of sexuality and dance are very strong, and I was not spared from them. When I first thought of taking ballet classes, I slightly worried about what people would think of me. What would my dad think?! Even one of the most feminist women I know commented to me that the men in the New York City Ballet were obviously all gay. I don't see that as obvious, but somehow someone quite versed in sexual politics did see it? Even when I did get over my worries, I wondered to myself if I would be the only straight man in ballet.

Fact: There are straight men in ballet and there are gay men in ballet. Deciding to take ballet, does not actually make a statement about your sexuality.

Many have tried to boost the amount of boy ballet dancers by promoting that it is really macho and athletic to jump around and lift girls up in the air. Yes, ballet takes a lot of strength and endurance, but it is not macho. It does not fit the skewed definition of masculinity described earlier, nor, by its nature will it ever. Some try to say that ballet is worth it because you get to be around all of the ladies. While it is nice to be around women for the amazing energy they give off, this idea is detrimental on two points. First, many men who want to do ballet are just as scared of being thought of as a creep as they are of being thought of as gay. Second, it marginalizes homosexual males who want to dance. Making ballet as an art and form of expression available to heterosexual dancers should not be done at the expense of homosexual male dancers.

The best solution I have seen to this dilemma comes from an article by Jennifer Fisher (2007). She provides a solution that does not have to redefine dancing for men in the article titled "Make it Maverick: Rethinking the 'Make it Macho' Strategy for Men in Ballet." Fisher points out that "Boys and men who do ballet must be either exceptionally brave or foolhardy, or both…because of the art form's strong associations with a super-feminized world," (p. 45). Most importantly, Fisher explains that the male dancer is someone who is a bit of rebel and doesn't care what everyone else thinks. She identifies some examples:

"The athletic boy who finds he is good at ballet accidentally and likes
   the unique and secure position this usually gives him;
The boy in a large family who stakes out unusual territory because his
   brothers and sisters have already claimed a lot of other professions;
Gay or straight men who do not worry about putting a macho reputation
   at stake;
Gay or straight men who find the arts a welcoming environment for
   many kinds of people;
      Secure men who do not worry what people think" (Fisher, 2007, p.
64).
Maybe you are worried a little bit about what people would think if you took
dance. But what do you care? Shake up their world, welcome them to a
reality where men dance and you can't do anything about it.

In short, go ahead and dance. Men have every right to just as much as
anybody.

References

Fisher, J. "Make it maverick: Rethinking the 'make it macho' strategy for
      men in ballet." Dance Chronicle. 30.1 (2007): 45-66.

INTRO TO APPAREL

TIGHTS

Men's tights are different from women's tights and don't let anyone tell you different. I've had a few small stores tell me that there is no difference, only to end up with a pair of tights that are almost see through. Men's tights are thicker, and it is a good thing because leg hair under tights is quite gross looking.

The default color of tights is black. There are many different colors of tights that are used for performances, or when a dancer just wants to wear something different.

DANCE BELTS

This is probably both the most confusing and most important part of a man's ballet attire. It is called a dance belt, but it is really just a sturdy thong. It is worn beneath your tights. No man should ever wear tights without a dance belt. You know how in tights you are supposed to see the leg muscles and definition? Well the dance belt keeps everyone from seeing the definition of your crotch. Wearing a thong is worth it to avoid that.

There are dance belts in full back (not thongs), but they are pretty much for younger boys. You don't want to dance around with panty lines in your tights, it would look really weird. A dance belt feels extremely odd at first. I won't try to describe how it feels, you can find out for yourself. But it takes about 2 hours to get used to it. The dance belt provides a lot of support for your manhood, and that becomes extremely valuable in ballet.

BALLET SHOES

I remember when I bought my first pair of ballet shoes. I had no idea how to sew the elastics on. I laugh when I look at them now, sewn all crazy. I'll go over how to do this properly. Ballet slippers are light shoes made of either canvas or leather and have thin leather soles. They are often referred to as ballet flats, as opposed to pointe shoes. Pointe shoes are the shoes that dancers wear when they dance on their toes. Classically, men don't dance on their toes (en pointe), but there are a lot of men that do practice it. Pointe is quite advanced, so you don't need to worry about pointe shoes for a while, if ever, just know you don't need them. Regular ballet slippers are what you'll use.

TOPS, SHIRTS, AND LEOTARDS

Leotards are like shirts that join together under your crotch. Kind of like a woman's one-piece bathing suit. This is so that the shirt doesn't ride up and come untucked. I prefer to wear a t-shirt or tank top, and I pretty much always do. I'll go over ways of keeping a shirt tucked in without having to wear a leotard.

TIGHTS

Where do I buy men's tights?

Men's ballet tights are available online, through dance-wear catalogs, and in many dance-wear stores. It can be helpful to purchase your tights from a store that can aid you in finding the right size. However, sometimes a smaller ballet apparel store won't be familiar with helping a male. I suggest that you try visiting a dance apparel store if there is one near where you live, particularly if you live in a larger city. Dance stores in large cities will have a better chance of catering to male dancers.

If you go into a dance store and they seem to be confused by a male ballet dancer, or they seem to be trying to offer you some tights that are not made for men, I suggest that you find somewhere else to buy or order online. I have run into a couple stores that are really trying to help, but just don't understand the difference between men and women's tights. Women's tights are too thin for men and they are too see-through. Men's tights are thicker and more like tight leggings than pantyhose. If a store recognizes that you need men's tights and they offer to order some for you, this is acceptable. It means that they probably know what you need, and again, they can help you with the sizing.

If you feel more comfortable ordering from a website or catalog, it is not hard to figure out your size. Your dance studio probably has ballet apparel catalogs (although there will probably be only one page for men's stuff, if you are even lucky), and many great apparel websites have sizing charts online (see resources at the end of this chapter). Refer to the manufacturer's sizing charts when you are choosing your tights. In stores these charts are often printed on the back of the tights' packaging.

How much do men's tights cost?

Men's ballet tights usually cost somewhere in between $15-$30 for each pair. There are definitely more expensive tights, if you want something that is very trendy or fashionable (see resources), but your basic tights will fall within this price range.

How many pairs of tights do I need?

If you are dancing just twice a week, you can probably get by with one pair of tights. If you dance more than that, it will be helpful to have at least two pairs. Having more than one pair will allow you to wash and dry a pair while you still have a pair to use. Over time you will surely accumulate quite a few pairs of tights.

How long do ballet tights last?

A decent pair of tights will last you several months if you use them a couple times a week and wash and take care of them properly. As tights get older they will start to wear and get some holes. The first holes usually show up in the feet of footed tights, similar to how a pair of socks gets holes.

What kind of tights do I buy?

Buy your tights according to the color and style recommendations of your dance studio. If they do not specify, I highly recommend a pair of black tights. Black is pretty much the default color for men's classes and practice.

There are a few different popular styles of men's tights available. Tights can be **footed, footless**, or **convertible**. *Footed* tights go right down over your feet, like those children's footie pajamas. *Footless* tights go down to your ankle, or stop even higher, somewhere between your knee and ankle. *Convertible* tights can be either footed or footless. They have a hole in the back of the ankle so that you can roll them up off of your feet if you want.

Footed tights are often used in performances. What you use in class will probably come down to a matter of preference. I personally prefer footless tights. They are cheaper and I find them more comfortable.

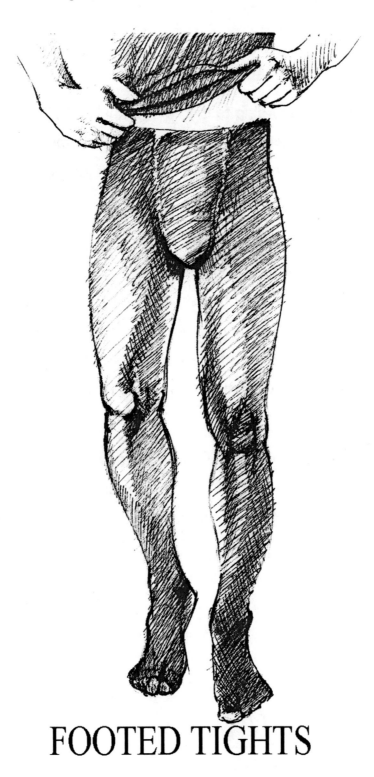

FOOTED TIGHTS

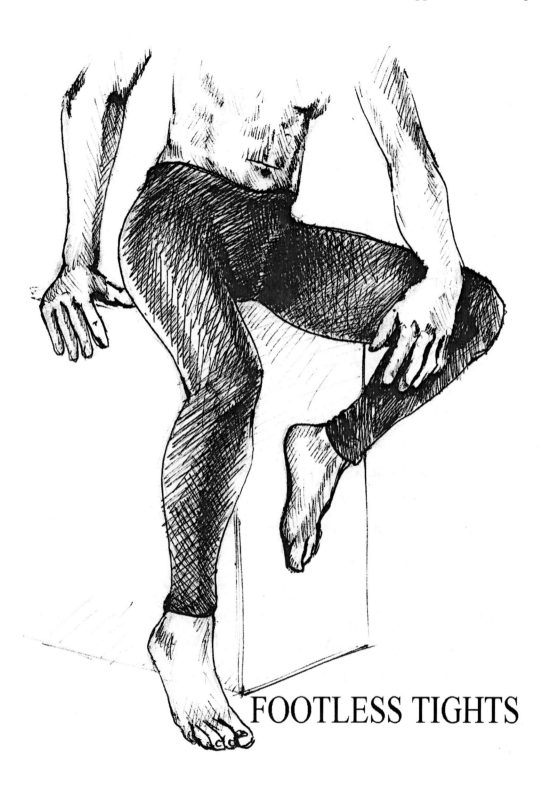

FOOTLESS TIGHTS

There are a few different brands that make men's tights. Most likely you will buy what you can, perhaps until you find a company that makes a pair you really like. See the resources at the end of this article for a list of some quality companies.

How do men wear ballet tights?

The most important thing that men must do when they wear ballet tights, is wear a dance belt underneath. See the chapter on dance belts.

How do I put tights on?

Putting tights on is pretty simple. The easiest way to do it is to roll up each leg of the tights before you stick your foot in. Don't just try to pull them on like a pair of pants. You may rip them, and they probably won't go on evenly. Roll up the leg by reaching your arm down to the bottom of the tights. If they are footless, grab the ankle, if they are footed, pinch to toes from the inside and pull them up to the waist of the tights. It is like you are pulling them inside-out, but stop before you get to the point where they would start becoming inside-out. Here you can stick your foot into the foot of the tights (or through the ankle if they're footless), and pull the tights up, releasing the bunches so that they go on pretty evenly.

PUTTING ON THE TIGHTS

You'll notice that once you have your tights on, and pull them all the way up, they can go high up. The waistband could probably go up to your chest. If you put the waistband around your waist, you'll probably notice that they might bunch around the crotch.

How do I keep my tights up?

You'll wan't your tights to be pulled up tight to your crotch, and be giving you a wedgie (you're already wearing the dance belt anyways). If it doesn't give you a wedgie, you'll get a uni-butt, which looks like you have one big butt-cheek and it looks weird and unnatural. Here are 2 good options for keeping your tights held up: **suspenders** or a **waist-belt**.

Tights can be ordered with *suspenders* on them, or you can put suspenders on your own pair. To put suspenders on your tights. Get some 1/2 inch or wider elastic. This is sold in many fabric and department stores. Put your tights on and pull them all the way up. Cut some pieces of elastic long enough to go from the front of your tights waist to the opposite side of your back tights waist. So you should have a piece go from your left side of your tights, below your left nipple, over your shoulder to your right side back, below your shoulder blade. Do the same thing from your right side, to your left back side. This will allow the suspenders to cross behind you, and keep them from slipping off of your shoulders. Mark the length of the elastic so that they are stretched, but not so tight they can't stretch anymore. Take your tights off and sew these elastics to the waist band just the way you measured them.

The problem with suspenders is that you have to wear your tights so high. You could wear them under a shirt, but then the elastic will rub on your bare chest. Find the softest elastic you can in this case. If you wear a shirt under the suspenders, you will have to tuck it in to your tights, which are pulled up really high, and that can look a little strange.

SUSPENDERS

The other option is to use a *waist-belt*. You can either use a thin belt you would use for your pants, or again, some elastic. My favorite method is to get a thick length of elastic, at least 1 inch thick and make a belt. Measure the length by pulling the elastic tight around the widest part of your hips. Pull it so tight you can't pull it anymore and add 2 inches to that length.

Cut that piece and use the 2 inch extra to overlap the ends of the elastic to make it a circle. Sew the two ends together at the overlap. Then put your tights on and pull them all the way up with the waist as high as it goes. Take your elastic belt you just made and step into it. Pull it all the way up (it will be tightest around your hips, but not so tight you can't pull it up). Pull the elastic up to be 1 inch below the waist of your tights. Roll the waistband of your tights over the elastic and then continue rolling it down, flipping over the elastic so that it wraps up the extra waist of tights. Keep pulling your tights up so that it stays tight in your crotch, and roll down until the elastic makes a waistband roll of tights that sits at a comfortable level. Instead of using the elastic, you can use a thin leather belt, but I find the elastic is easiest to use. This method creates a thicker waistband around your tights, but it still allows you to tuck in your shirt, holds your tights up, and looks pretty decent.

MEASURING THE ELASTIC

ROLLING THE WAISTBAND

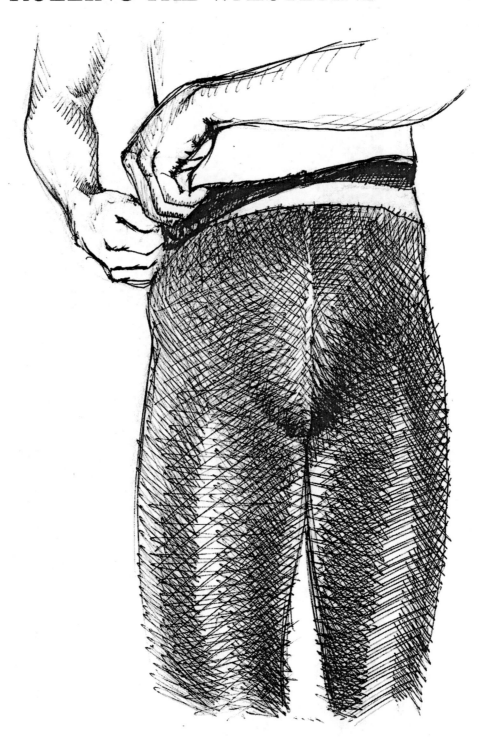

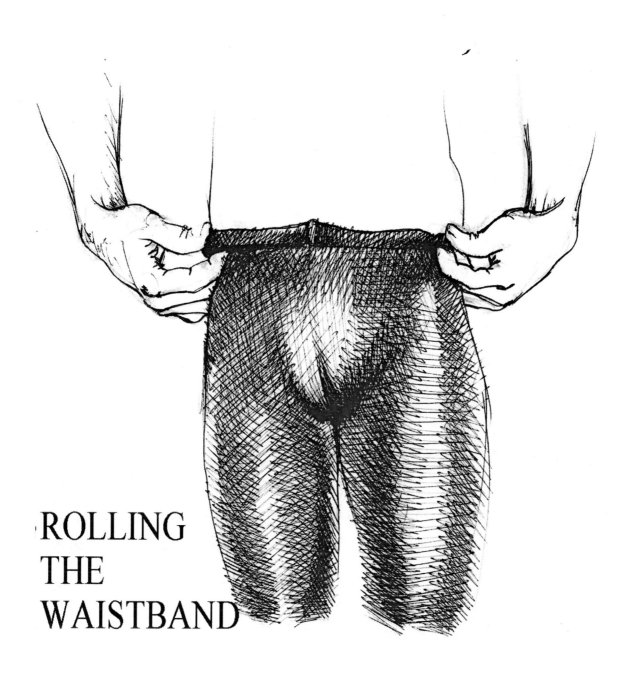

ROLLING THE WAISTBAND

Taking care of your tights

How do I clean my tights?

It is best to hand-wash your tights, but you can also wash them on a gentle cycle in a washing machine. People often say that hand-washing your tights will extend the life of them, but if you are dancing a lot, you will probably damage your tights more from dance than washing in the machine. However, when washing tights in a machine, you can often be left with soap residue on your tights, which you can shake or wipe off after they have dried. It may come as a shock to you if you grab a washed pair of tights and throw them on that you have white powdery soap streaks all over your tights. Some tights may be subject to this more than others. Washing your tights in a loose mesh bag can also prevent them from getting tangled in other items.

Leave your tights to hang dry. Dryers can be more damaging than your washing machine. It can take more than a day for your tights to hang dry, so plan ahead, especially if you only have one pair, or are washing all of your tights. It is awkward to go to ballet without tights, but it is possibly more uncomfortable to wear tights that haven't fully dried.

How often do I wash my tights?

Wash them whenever you get a chance. Maybe more often than that. Your tights get pretty intimate with all of your sweatiest areas, and you better be sweating in ballet. Get tights washing on your schedule, probably your weekly schedule. If you take 2 classes a week, you could have one pair and wash them every week. If you take 4 classes a week, maybe you should have 2 pairs and wash them once a week. No one will get mad or think less of you if your tights are always clean. You don't really want to smell in ballet class.

How do I take care of my tights and what about holes?

The first sign of aging tights is a hole. It doesn't take long for an unattended hole to turn into a big hole. The worst place to get a hole is in the butt or crotch, for obvious reasons. While some holes can be sewn, I usually retire a pair if I get a hole there. Even sewing a hole is temporary, and most likely when that sew rips, you will be left with an even bigger hole. I would rather buy a new pair of tights than expose my dance belt. If the hole is on the knee or leg, I will usually stitch it up. I like to use dental floss to stitch with, because it is strong, cheap, and easier for me handle than a tiny thread. I stitch across the hole just how a doctor stitches skin back together. To make the stitch less obvious, I usually color the floss in black with a marker. Stitching a hole will keep the hole from getting bigger right away, but the hole will probably come back. You might want to start saving for a new pair of tights.

On footed tights, you will get a hole in the feet pretty fast. When the holes get too big, I usually cut the feet off and roll up the ankle, turning them into a pair of footless tights. When those tights get a hole in the leg, I'll cut them into shorts and use them in hot summer classes. It helps to save a little bit of money.

Tights Resources

DANCE APPAREL

The Ballet For Men Store – Dance Apparel - http://astore.amazon.com/balletformen-20

MotionWear Dancewear - http://www.motionwearstore.com/collections-dance-mens-apparel/collections-dance-mens-apparel.asp

Discount Dance Supply - http://www.discountdance.com

QUALITY TIGHTS COMPANIES

MStevens - http://mstevens-dancewear.com/main.html

Capezio - http://www.capeziostore.com/category-s/122.htm

Eurotard - https://www.eurotard.com/catalog/default.aspx?ID=68

Leo's Dancewear - http://www.leosdancewear.com

COOL TIGHTS

Yumiko - http://store.yumiko-online.com/guys-en.html

We Love Colors - http://www.welovecolors.com/Shop/MensTights.htm
(only the professional tights are wearable for ballet)

DANCE
BELT

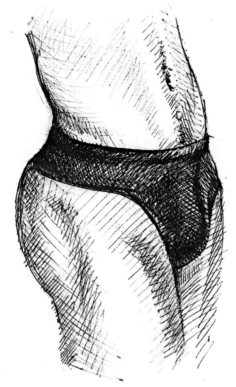

FRONT OF DANCE BELT

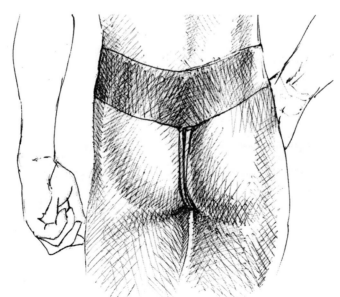

BACK OF DANCE BELT

What is a Dance Belt?

The dance belt is one of the mysteries of men's ballet. It is extremely important, but it is hard to find information on what the heck it is. If you are going to wear tights, you *need* to wear a dance belt.

The dance belt is worn under your tights. You don't wear underwear, you wear the dance belt, then the tights on top of that. The dance belt serves two main purposes. It serves as your support and stability for your "manhood". You are going to be doing a lot of moving around, but there is one part of you that would do better staying still. The dance belt is designed to do that. The other purpose it serves, is to keep everything from being too visible. The contours of muscles are often on display in ballet, but not in this area. The dance belt will provide you with more of a bulge, than a discernible outline.

Buying a Dance Belt

Knowing that you need a dance belt is step 1. Good job, you got one of the hardest parts over. Now you have to actually get one. They cost about $15 to $25. If you have visited a dance store, and they seem to know a little bit about men's stuff, you can check with them about a dance belt. Dance belts are available online (see resources at the end of this chapter).

Sizing is based on your waist size. Check the manufacturer's charts before ordering. You want to get a dance belt that is closest to your skin color. They usually come in tan, black, and white. White is probably not suitable for anyone. Tan and black are closer to actual skin tones. Loosely matching the color to your skin tone will keep them from being obvious beneath a lighter pair of tights.

Wearing a Dance Belt

The dance belt is a thong. You'll have to get over the shock. If you want to be a ballet dancer, it is what you'll have to get used to. There are dance belts that are not thongs, full back dance belts, but they are usually for younger children. The dance belt has to be a thong in order to provide enough support, and to not have any panty-lines.

The first time you put it on, it will probably be uncomfortable. Within about two-hours you'll be used to it. You get used to it, but it doesn't mean you're going to be shopping for man-thongs in the men's department.

Taking Care of your Dance Belt

Your dance belt will get as sweaty as a jock strap. Wash it after every use. It is easy enough to wash them by hand, since you probably won't be doing laundry after every dance class. Getting into a habit of washing your dance belt as you prepare your shower will help you keep a clean one available. You will most likely need to have 2 or more dance belts and keep them on rotation. After you wash them, fold it up and squeeze out the water. Hang it up to dry in your closet or somewhere out of the way. It will take a day or two to dry, so keep in mind when you have your next class. I have to wash one a couple days in advance, having two drying and one clean ready to go.

The dance belt is just a part of being a male ballet dancer. You'll get used to it. It will help you move and dance just like the other apparel does.

Dance Belt Resources

The Ballet For Men Store – Dance Apparel - http://astore.amazon.com/
balletformen-20

Discount Dance Supply - http://www.discountdance.com

BALLET SHOES

BALLET SHOES

I got my first pair of ballet shoes after I had taken a few ballet classes. I knew that I wanted to keep taking ballet, so it was time for me to invest in some apparel. The first piece of ballet apparel I got was my ballet shoes. I had been wearing socks for my first few classes, and it didn't take long for my feet to start to get sore in class. I went to a small dance wear store in the town I lived in at the time. They didn't have any men's shoes, but they did measure my feet and order a pair for me. They were a pair of white leather slippers. When it came time to sew them, I had no idea what to do. I know how to sew, but I didn't know where to sew the elastics. I didn't know anyone who could tell me how to do it either. So they ended up really crooked. They look pretty funny, but it wasn't too long before they got wore out and I sewed my next pair right.

Choosing Men's Ballet Shoes

Ballet shoes are sometimes referred to as slippers, ballet flats or flat shoes, as opposed to pointe shoes or toe shoes. Pointe shoes are the shoes that dancers wear when they dance on their toes. These are for advanced dancers, and men are never really asked to do it. Some guy dancers do dance on pointe, but typically because they want to. Many professional male dancers may never dance on pointe. It is typically reserved for women, especially in performances. Not to say you can't do pointe, you just can't do it right now, and will probably never be required to do it.

Ballet shoes, the flat kind that you will need, come with a couple different styles of sole. They can be either a split sole, or full sole. This refers to the leather bottom of the shoe. On a full sole it runs all the way along the bottom of the shoe. On the split sole, there are two separate leather pads, one under the heel, and one under the balls of the feet. The split sole are the most common shoes. They may be the only ones you will find, but if you have a choice, you might as well go with the split sole and get used to using them. Full sole shoes are generally for young beginners.

Ballet slippers are usually made out of either canvas or leather. Canvas shoes are very common. They are lighter, softer, and cheaper. Leather shoes can last a bit longer, but considering that canvas shoes might be a bit more comfortable, and are typically half the price, I suggest going with canvas slippers.

You can also choose the color of your slippers. Black or white are most common. You may decide based on what your studio suggests or what their dress policy is. Slippers also come in tan, or you can dye a pair of white slippers almost any color you desire with some Rit dye. Shoes also come in pink, but as you can guess, those are usually worn by the girls.

Sizing Men's Ballet Shoes

Some companies size their ballet slippers according to street shoe size. Some base their size on centimeters. If you go to a store to buy your shoes, they should be able to fit you, or will have you try on different pairs and help you find the right size. If you order them online or from a catalog, there should be a sizing chart that will tell you what shoes to order based on your street shoe size.

Buying the Slippers

If you would like to order online, you can find your shoes in the Ballet For Men Store, Discount Dance, or Fuzi Dance, to name a few places. I stopped by the Fuzi warehouse the other day and they had many larger sizes of shoes for men, even in narrow, medium, and wide.

Sewing Your New Ballet Shoes

It isn't really that hard to sew your slippers once you know where the elastics go. You will need the following:

- ballet shoes
- sturdy needle
- thread or dental floss
- pen
- black marker (for black shoes)

The shoes already have one end of each of the two thick elastics sewn to the back of the shoe. You are going to put the shoe on, and cross the elastics over your foot to the seam that is in the middle of the shoe, by the arch of your foot.

Pull the elastics snug, but not too tight. They should be stretched just a bit. Mark on both elastics with a pen where it meets the top of the shoe.

BALLET SHOES

SEAM

ELASTIC

See the seams here. The elastics should be brought to this point on the shoe. Take the shoe off and line the elastic up with your mark at the top of the shoe. This time you want the elastic on the inside of the shoe though. So the elastics should be criss-crossed, but they should not be twisted. Sew one elastic to one side, by stitching the floss through the elastic and the shoe, but stay beneath the black trim on the top of the shoe. There is another elastic running around inside there, and you might not be able to tighten the shoe later if you sew through it.

Sew both sides with enough stitches that it feels like it will hold really well and tie off the ends of your your thread. Cut off the leftover thread, and trim the excess elastic.

Once you've sewn and trimmed both sides, put the shoe back on. The other elastics that cross at the front will tighten the opening of the shoe. You want to pull those tight, but again, not too tight, just snug. If they are too tight, the back of the shoe will dig into your heel. You are going to tie a bow, just like you tie your shoe. It would probably do best to double knot it.

Take the shoe back off. Turn the front part of the shoe inside out. Use a piece of masking tape to tape the bow to the inside of the top of the shoe.

Turn the shoe back right-side-out. Use the marker to write your name on the inside somewhere. Also use it to color in the thread so it won't be visible on the outside of the shoe.
Repeat all of this onto the other shoe, and you're done!

If you don't have time to sew your shoes, and you only really need them for practice or rehearsal, there is another way to make your shoes work. You can tie the ends of the elastics together. Put the shoe on and tie the bow like you normally would with the smaller elastics. Tuck it in. Take your big elastic loop and twist it once to make a loop to slip over the front of your foot. This will hold your shoe in place, but it won't look as good as a sewn shoe, or be as comfortable.

Taking Care of Your Ballet Shoes

Your ballet shoes will get pretty sweaty. You'll want to wash them so they don't stink too much. They are easy to hand wash and hang dry. It would be best to wash them and dry them inside out. Keep in mind that it will take a day or two for the shoes to dry. You could throw them in the washer and dryer, but like all other ballet apparel, this will cut down on their lifespan. Washing and drying shoes can cause a rip or a fray to become a hole that will just keep getting bigger.

Replacing Your Ballet Shoes

How long your shoes last will depend on how much you are dancing. If you are taking class or dancing everyday, they may be worn out in 2 months or less. If you are dancing only a couple days a week, your shoes could last much longer. You will probably need a new pair of shoes for each performance, so that they look nice and new on stage. If you are just practicing, you can use your shoes until you've worn holes right through. Once your toe shows it is probably time to get a new pair!

POINTE SHOES

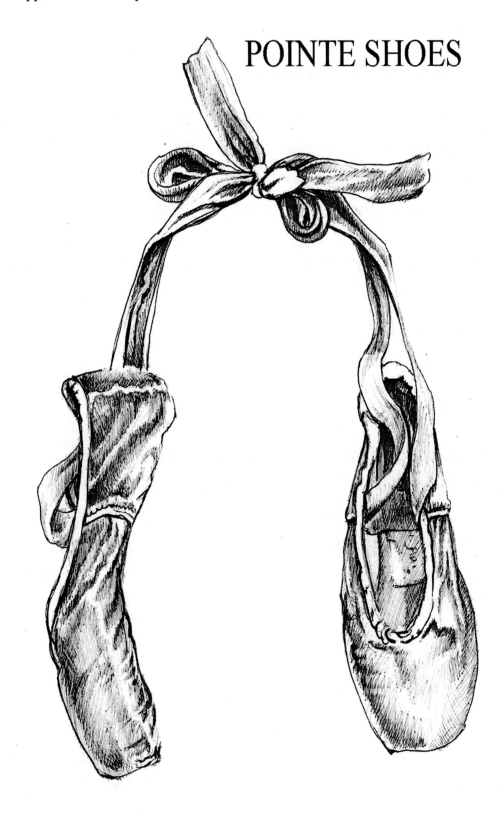

A Little Bit About Pointe Shoes

Pointe shoes are one of the most famous pieces of attire in ballet. Pointe shoes have a strong, boxy front (called a box) which enables the dancer to balance on their toes. The heel of the shoes are secured by ribbons around the ankle. Pointe shoes are much more expensive than flat shoes. They can typically cost around $70.

The first thing you should know is that pointe shoes are not for beginners. Dancers do not start taking pointe until they have developed enough technique and strength to prevent injury. Even dancers who start ballet at a very young age, will often not go on pointe until they are around 12 years old, sometimes older.

The second thing you should know is that guys do not typically dance on pointe. I say typically, but that does not mean that guys can't. Traditionally it is the female dancer that dances on pointe, the male staying on flat. In partnering, it is usually the girl who is on her toes, while the guy helps to support her and lift her. There are few traditional performances that require a male to dance on pointe.

However, there are many guys who decide to learn pointe. Dancing on pointe takes a lot of dedication, but is amazingly beautiful. A lot of guys desire to learn pointe because they enjoy expressing themselves in that style. Learning pointe can also help guys to build a tremendous amount of leg and foot strength, develop stronger foot technique, and better balance. Knowing how to dance pointe can also give guys a better sense of what the female partner requires in partnering. A guy who understands pointe could more quickly understand how to get a girl on balance, or keep her on balance during turns.

Still, a majority of male dancers never dance on pointe. The main reason is that there is a lack of performance opportunities for male pointe dancers. One of the few consistent opportunities for males to dance on pointe is the comedic, Les Ballets Trockadero Des Monte Carlo (www.trockadero.org), also known as "The Trocks." This parody ballet company features male dancers dressed as female ballerinas. While the Trocks are extremely talented, not all male dancers who dance on pointe want to dance in comedic drag.

Male pointe dancers will also have trouble finding shoes that are big enough for their feet, or that are not pink. If a guy's feet are too big, they will have to usually special order a pair of pointe shoes. If they don't want pink shoes, they may have to dye them or color them black with a marker.

Although dancing on pointe may strengthen feet and legs, and give guys a sense of the typically female side of partnering, learning pointe is so intense that it is often easier for men to find other ways build strength and technique. By continuing to practice partnering, male dancers will get a sense of what the girl on pointe requires.

As a male dancer, you will never be expected to dance on pointe. This comes as a relief to many male dancers, but some will still decide they want to learn. I admire these men and encourage them to continue exploring what interests them.

If you are interested in learning more about pointe, there are plenty of websites dedicated to information for girls, where you can find the basics. In an effort to support all male dancers, I will in time try to find and create more resources for male pointe dancers.

TOPS

The most common tops for ballet apparel are leotards or shirts. Since you will be moving around so much, you'll want a top that will stay in place and not come untucked or pull up. Leotards are like shirts that connect between the legs to hold it down. If you get the right shirt you should be able to make it so it won't come untucked, I'll tell you how. Unless you want to wear a leotard, you won't ever need to unless it is required for a performance.

Shirts

Plain white t-shirts, such as Hanes or Fruit of the Loom are suitable for dance classes. You can buy packs of undershirts for pretty cheap, so these are useful, especially if you are dancing a few days a week or more. You'll want to get a size that is tight fitting, but comfortable. Tighter shirts will show the position of your upper body better, and this is important for class. It is similar to the reason you wear tights. The dance teacher will be able to see if you are properly positioned. If a shirt is too baggy, the instructor will have a harder time giving you corrections.

Baggier shirts will also be harder to tuck in. Tucking a shirt in to the waistband of your dance belt should be enough to keep it from pulling out while you dance. If the shirt is fitted close enough, you will prevent having your shirt bunch up under your tights. This works well with the rolled down waist band that I talked about in the tights section. If you are wearing tights with suspenders, you may want to wear the shirt on the outside, over your tights and suspenders.

Sleeveless shirts and tank tops are also great for practicing in. You will probably notice more freedom in your arms and shoulders when you wear a sleeveless top. There are also a nice variety of tank tops and sleeveless shirts for when you are sick of wearing a plain t-shirt. If you like more breathable fitness and sport oriented shirts, Under Armour and Lululemon make nice shirts, but they are much more expensive than plain t-shirts.

T-SHIRT

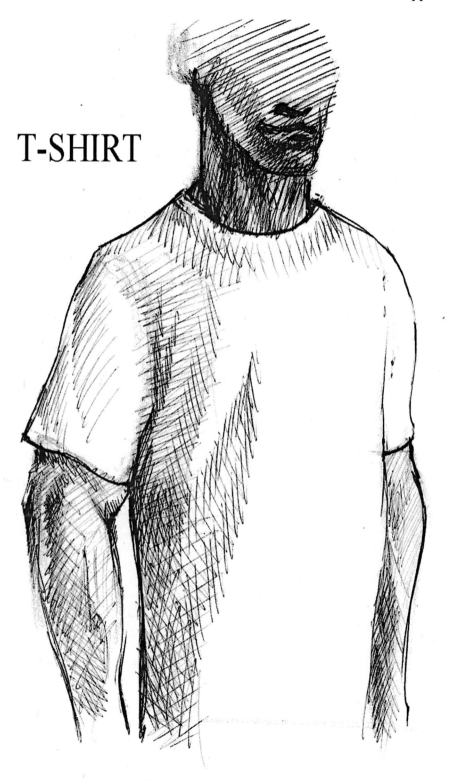

Leotards

Leotards are made for men and women. Women typically wear their tights under their leotard, but men's leotards are made to be worn under the tights. This way it looks like it is just a shirt. Leotards for men are often made with a thong back, similar to dance belts, to prevent lines and provide adequate support. Some leotards may contain snaps beneath the crotch in order to put it on. But you'll notice most leotards for men have a scoop neck. This is because the leotard is put on by stepping through the neck-hole and pulling it on.

There are also unitards, which are a combination of tights and top. Similar to this are biketards. Those are one-piece shorts and top. They look kind of like wrestling uniforms.

For ballet practice you will either choose what to wear based on the studio's dress code, or if there is not a strict policy, you will wear what you feel most comfortable in. It is helpful to know of the different types of apparel, or the different ways it can be worn. Different performances may require you to wear new types of costumes.

LEOTARD

Tops Resources

The Ballet For Men Store – Dance Apparel - http://astore.amazon.com/
balletformen-20

Discount Dance Supply - http://www.discountdance.com

Lululemon Store - http://shop.lululemon.com

RESOURCES

Tights Resources

DANCE APPAREL

The Ballet For Men Store – Dance Apparel - http://astore.amazon.com/balletformen-20

MotionWear Dancewear - http://www.motionwearstore.com/collections-dance-mens-apparel/collections-dance-mens-apparel.asp

Discount Dance Supply - http://www.discountdance.com

QUALITY TIGHTS COMPANIES

MStevens - http://mstevens-dancewear.com/main.html

Capezio - http://www.capeziostore.com/category-s/122.htm

Eurotard - https://www.eurotard.com/catalog/default.aspx?ID=68

Leo's Dancewear - http://www.leosdancewear.com

COOL TIGHTS

Yumiko - http://store.yumiko-online.com/guys-en.html

We Love Colors - http://www.welovecolors.com/Shop/MensTights.htm

(only the professional tights are wearable for ballet)

Dance Belt Resources

The Ballet For Men Store – Dance Apparel - http://astore.amazon.com/balletformen-20

Discount Dance Supply - http://www.discountdance.com

Ballet Shoe Resources

Discount Dance Supply - http://www.discountdance.com

Fuzi Dance – http://www.fuzi.net

Tops Resources

The Ballet For Men Store – Dance Apparel - http://astore.amazon.com/balletformen-20

Discount Dance Supply - http://www.discountdance.com

Lululemon Store - http://shop.lululemon.com

BALLETFORMEN.COM

Ballet For Men is a website encouraging men to dance.

BalletForMen.com provides:

- tutorials

- free downloads

- podcasts

- book and video reviews

- apparel

Get BalletForMen.com T-shirts!

BALLET T-SHIRTS

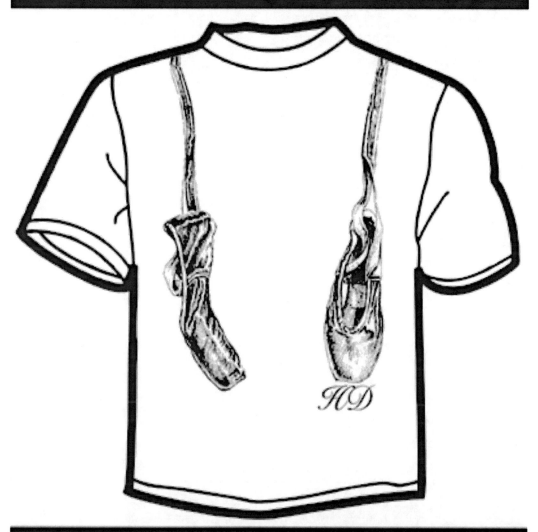

HDWEAR.COM

CPSIA information can be obtained at www.ICGtesting.com
Printed in the USA
LVOW10s1928030116

468919LV00004B/37/P